The Dictionary of Ordinary EXTRAORDINARY ANIMALS

by Lisa McGuinness and Leslie Jonath

illustrated by Lisa Congdon

RP|KIDS
PHILADELPHIA · LONDON

To my extraordinary nieces, Monique and Sarah.
—Leslie

For my son, Jordan, who loves wild and wacky animal facts.
—Lisa

Books published by Running Press are available at special discounts for bulk purchases in the United
States by corporations, institutions, and other organizations. For more information, please contact the
Special Markets Department at the Perseus Books Group, 2300 Chestnut Street, Suite 200, Philadelphia,
PA 19103, or call (800) 810-4145, ext. 5000, or e-mail special.markets@perseusbooks.com.

ISBN 978-0-7624-4063-4

Library of Congress Control Number: 2010935841

9 8 7 6 5 4 3 2 1
Digit on the right indicates the number of this printing

Cover design and interior design by Sara Gillingham
Edited by Marlo Scrimizzi
Typography: Duality and Otari

Published by Running Press Kids
an imprint of Running Press Book Publishers
A Member of the Perseus Books Group
2300 Chestnut Street
Philadelphia, PA 19103-4371

Visit us on the web!
www.runningpress.com

HAVE YOU EVER WONDERED about the difference between a hare and a rabbit? Did you know that a hummingbird can fly upside down and backwards, or that a platypus has venom like a rattlesnake? You might be interested to learn that your goldfish will grow, and grow, and grow, as long as you keep increasing the size of its tank!

From the way they sleep, sing, or dance—all critters have something that is uniquely fascinating and fun to learn. Chock full of amazing facts about the wild, the woolly, the creepy, the crawly, and the sea worthy, this book gives you the inside scoop about our favorite curious animals, from A to Z. We hope this book will entice you to look more closely at all the creatures on our planet and to appreciate the unique adaptations and behaviors that make every animal truly extraordinary!

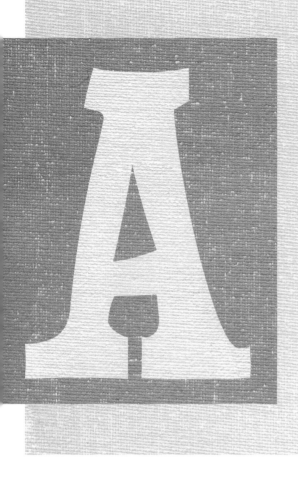

Aardvark

Also called earth pigs, these fuzzy animals resemble both a pig and a kangaroo, though they are not related to either.

Aardvarks live in Africa, south of the Sahara Desert. They are nocturnal animals: They sleep during the day in cool underground burrows and then hunt at night for termites. They have long, shovel-like claws for digging through the large, earthen termite mounds, and they can close the nostrils of their piglike snouts so no dust or bugs sneak in. Another name aardvarks earned is "ant bear," because they use the same techniques to raid underground ant nests.

FUN FACT

One difference between alligators and crocodiles is that alligators have U-shaped jaws, while crocs have V-shaped jaws. Also, the fourth tooth on the lower jaws stick up over a crocodile's lips, but not so for alligators.

Alligator

These predators look sluggish and clumsy on land, but once they slip into water, they're agile and fast. The American alligator is found mostly in Florida and Louisiana. Hungry gators will eat just about anything, such as fish, turtles, snakes, and small mammals. But it's very rare that they eat humans.

Scientists believe that alligators have been around for more than 150 million years. No wonder their skin is so wrinkly!

Male alligators grow 10 to 15 feet long and weigh up to 1,000 pounds! Female alligators grow to almost 10 feet. Offspring are hatched from eggs, which is why baby alligators are called hatchlings.

Anaconda

The stealth anaconda is the fattest snake in the world. There are four species of anaconda including the Bolivian, yellow, and dark-spotted anacondas, but the biggest is the green anaconda, which on average weighs 350 pounds and reaches more than 25 feet long—more than the length of a swimming pool.

These constrictors don't use venom to kill their prey. Instead, like a boa, they wrap their body around their victim and squeeze to cut off its air. In addition to fish, turtles, and rodents, anacondas devour large animals, such as wild pigs, deer, and even jaguars! After large meals, anacondas can go for weeks without food.

FUN FACT

The anaconda's eyes and nose are on top of its head, which allows it to breathe and see while almost completely submerged.

Angelfish

These dazzling, heavenly fish are beautiful!
Found all over the world, angelfish live in
both fresh and saltwater as long as the water
is warm. The queen angelfish is one of the
most beautiful saltwater species, with a blue
body and a bright yellow tail, spotted with
bits of purple and orange. Another saltwater
species, the emperor angelfish, has scales
that form a blue maze. Freshwater angelfish
are equally diverse in color and patterns. All
angelfish have distinctive, long upper and
lower fins that flow behind them like angel's
robes or wings.

Ant

These teeny insects
have superhero
strength for their
size. Ants can lift
20 times their body
weight!

Ants don't have
ears—but they can
"hear" by feeling
vibrations in the
ground through their
sensitive feet.

Ants live in colo-
nies with millions of
other ants including
the queen, male, and
female workers. The
queen's job is to lay
eggs, and the male's
job to mate with her.
The female workers
gather food, attack
enemy ants, and care
for the babies.

FUN FACT

The main difference between an ape and a monkey is that monkeys have tails and apes do not!

Ape

Apes are the largest of all primates! Primates are mammals with forward facing eyes, hands, and hand-like feet. Chimpanzees, orangutans, bonobos, and gorillas are all apes.

Chimpanzees are able to use tools, orangutans use large leaves as umbrellas, and gorillas laugh and make play faces when they're having fun. Ape territory is the rain forest, where they live in complex social groups and families.

Even though apes are hairy, they don't have whiskers and their ears are relatively small. They have eyes that see in color and opposable thumbs—which move independently of the fingers used to grip onto things. Also like people, they have fingernails.

Armadillo

The aramadillo, named after the Spanish word for "little armored one," has bony plates that cover its back, head, legs, and tail. This armor does much to protect armadillos from pokes and bites. Some can tuck their heads and legs into their shells, and curve into balls to protect themselves.

These slow-moving animals sleep as much as 16 hours each day and come out only to forage for food at dawn and dusk. Their long, sticky tongues help them slurp up beetles, termites, and other insects. Of the 20 armadillo species, only one lives in the United States. The rest live in Latin America.

FUN FACT

The nine-banded armadillo alwasys gives birth to exactly four identical babies from one egg.

B

Bandicoot

These tiny, furry, mouselike animals are often mistaken for rodents, but they are actually small marsupials (like kangaroos)! What makes a marsupial unique is that their babies are born not quite fully formed. Baby bandicoots emerge tiny (less than a half inch long!), hairless, and blind, and crawl into their mother's pouch, where they drink milk while they grow. When the babies are fully developed, they emerge from the pouch and begin life on their own.

Bandicoots eat both animals and plants, including worms, centipedes, roots, grasses, berries, and seeds.

FUN FACT

The name *bandicoot* translates from its roots in a language from India as "pig-rat."

Bat

These nocturnal creatures are active and sleep during the day while dangling upside down! There are about 1,000 different species of bats, which can be divided into two main categories: fruit bats, which feed on fruit and pollen, and carnivorous bats, which feed mainly on insects. Vampire bats really do drink blood! But they rarely kill their prey, and the bite is often so delicate that the animal whose blood they're slurping rarely even notices!

Bats are the only mammals that can fly. At night, many bats use echolocation to navigate. Their sound waves bounce off their prey to determine where and in which direction it is moving.

FUN FACT

Beavers have clear eyelids, in addition to regular eyelids, which act as goggles when they are in the water!

Beaver

Using only their big, strong teeth, these busy animals can "saw" through a tree! Then they use these trees to build dams so big they can change the course of streams, and flood fields.

"Lodge" is the name for the mud, bark, branch, and grass dens that beavers call home. They build an entrance underwater and a second story above water that stays dry, which is where the beavers sleep. Beavers often use the same lodge year after year and will continue to add onto it.

Beavers are excellent swimmers and use their long, webbed feet like swimming fins and paddle-shaped tails to steer. Their fur is oily and waterproof so they stay warm in very cold water and don't need to hibernate in the winter.

Bee

FUN FACT

In hot weather, bees collect water to keep the hive cool.

Bees are responsible for more than just honey! They buzz from flower to flower, collecting nectar and pollinating plants along the way. A bee will visit between 50 and 100 flowers in a single day and can carry more than half her weight in pollen! Bees share the locations of pollen sources with each other with a dance called the "waggle dance."

Bees are not very speedy, and are slower than most other insects. They try to keep out of the rain, because if a bee's wings get wet, it has a difficult time flying.

Most bees live together in hives, organized into complex social groups. The most powerful bee is the queen bee. She lays eggs to populate the hive. The worker bees are female. They maintain the hive but they don't reproduce. Male bees are called drones, and their only job is to mate with the queen.

Black Bear

Black bears are solitary creatures. They are excellent walkers and talented swimmers. They are fast runners, too, although after feasting all summer to prepare for winter, bears get fat, and therefore get hot and tired quickly when they run!

Bears often roam for miles and miles while foraging for food especially roots, berries, insects, fish, small mammals, and, yes, honey!

Bears spend the spring, summer, and fall eating to bulk up for winter so that when they hibernate they can live off their body fat. The colder the climate, the longer they snooze away the winter.

FUN FACT

Ever hear of a *white* black bear? Believe it or not, black bears can be brown, blond, gray, black, and yes, white.

Blowfish

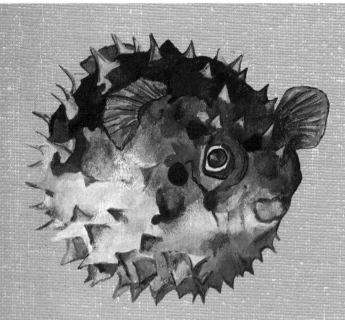

These elastic fish can instantly expand into round balls. When these sneaky tricksters want to fool predators, they quickly fill their stomachs with water, blowing themselves up to several times their normal size. When inflated, their skin becomes tight and tough, so the fish appear inedible. There are more than 120 species of blowfish. Blowfish are also known as puffer fish. They come in many different colors and shapes, but most of them live in the tropics and are extremely poisonous to eat.

FUN FACT

Blowfish are so toxic, one fish has enough poison in it to kill 30 adult humans—and there is no known cure!

Boa Constrictor

Like anacondas, these slithery reptiles put the squeeze on their prey. Boa constrictors are not poisonous, but they have jaws lined with small, hooked teeth. Boas can open their jaws so wide they can even swallow monkeys and small pigs!

While they are excellent swimmers, boas like to stay on dry land and live in burrows or hollow logs. Boa constrictors can grow to be more than 13 feet long and can weigh up to 100 pounds when fully grown! Female boas incubate eggs in their bodies and can hatch up to 60 baby boa constrictors at a time!

Butterfly

These brightly colored, winged insects begin their lives as caterpillars, before going through metamorphosis and emerging as butterflies. Once out in the world, butterflies rarely eat! However they drink water by sipping through hollow, strawlike tongues.

Butterflies are strong flyers and can zoom up to 30 miles per hour and reach surprising heights: Some butterflies have been seen flying by tall buildings more than 1,000 feet in the air! If they get caught in a windstorm, they can be moved as far as 100 miles a day.

Butterflies are cold-blooded, so they rely on the sun to keep them warm. Butterflies can't close their eyes and don't actually sleep, but they try to find a warm, dry place to rest during the night.

FUN FACT

The main behavioral difference between moths and butterflies is that butterflies fly during the day and most moths fly at night!

FUN FACT

Boas love to eat bats! They lurk in trees and nab them from the air.

Camel

These lumpy animals come in two distinct shapes: with one hump or two.

Contrary to what many people think, a camel's hump isn't filled with water—it is filled with fat! Camels can slurp around 30 gallons in one drinking session! Which is how these amazing beasts can go a week or more without drinking and long periods without food! Camels close their nostrils to keep blowing sand out of their noses.

Like a beaver's, their eyes have a clear inner eyelid that protects them while still allowing them to see. They also have double rows of extra-long eyelashes that shield their eyes from swirling sand.

FUN FACT

Camels have wide pads on their feet to keep them from sinking into the sand.

Caterpillar

These creepy crawlers come in an array of colors and shapes—including green and plump, brown and hairy, and even horned. This camouflaging helps them hide from predators. In addition to blending into the background, caterpillars have other tricks to fend off attacks. They hide in rolled leaves, spit at their enemies, and some even play dead!

The process caterpillars go through to become moths or butterflies is called metamorphosis. Metamorphosis starts with the podlike stage called a pupa (if the caterpillar is changing into a moth) or a chrysalis (if it's changing into a butterfly). The amount of time the caterpillar spends transforming varies depending on the species. It can be as short as nine days or as long as one year!

FUN FACT

Aquatic caterpillars have gills and can live under water.

Chameleon

Chameleons are the lizard version of a mood ring: They turn different colors depending on light, temperature, and emotion.

While there are many species, all chameleons are characterized by flattened bodies and bulging, independently moving eyes. Some have crests, horns, or spines. The males use horns or spines to defend their territories and to help them attract a mate—which is when they turn the brightest colors, as well.

Chameleons have unique toes that are bunched together on the side of each foot. Their long tails are often used to grasp tree limbs.

FUN FACT

Some species of chameleons have tongues that are longer than their bodies!

Clownfish

These brightly colored fish, with distinct white markings, make their homes in poisonous, fish-eating anemones! The skin of clownfish is covered in a layer of mucus, making them immune to the anemone's sting. When choosing an anemone to live in, a clownfish circles and touches its tentacles until the two become familiar.

Clownfish live in groups, or schools, led by one female. She is the largest fish in the group. Along with the one chosen breeding male, she is the only one in the school to have babies, which hatch from eggs. When the female fish in the school dies, her mate changes himself into a female! Then another male in the group becomes her mate.

FUN FACT

The black "tear streak" that runs from eyes to mouth helps protect cheetah's eyes from the glare.

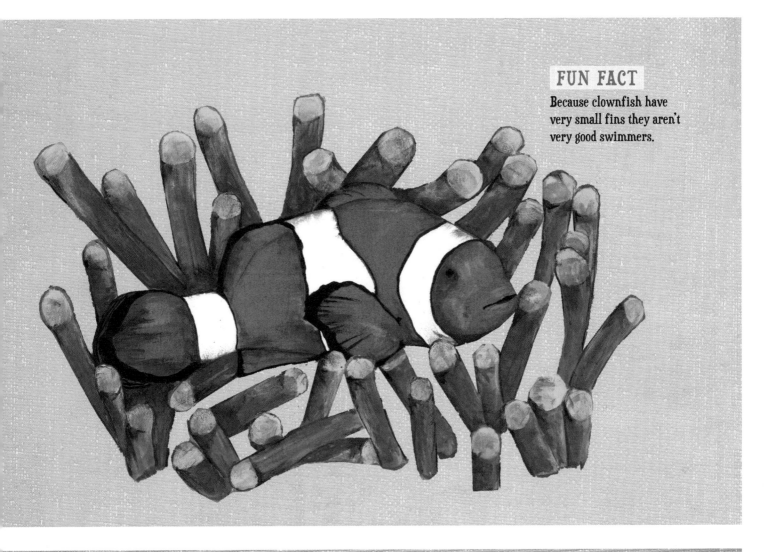

Cheetah

These speedy cats are the fastest land animals. Cheetahs can accelerate up to 60 miles per hour in only three seconds—faster than most cars! Their long and lanky bodies have flexible spines that allow their front legs to stretch way in front of them, creating a huge speed-efficient stride. They move so quickly that their bodies are entirely off the ground more than half the time they are running. Cheetahs can change course in midair.

While cheetahs are exceptionally quick, they cannot keep up their speed for very long. In fact, most cheetah sprints last for less than a minute.

Cobra

FUN FACT

When baby cobras emerge from their eggs, they are approximately 18 to 20 inches long and have enough venom to kill a grown human!

When confronted, these dramatic, poisonous snakes flatten their necks to make an unusual shape. The most famous cobra is the king cobra. King cobras can raise their bodies up to one-third of their length, while moving forward to attack—allowing them to look a six-foot-tall person right in the eye! They also hiss to send out a warning, and any animal or person who does not heed the warning should beware, because king cobras are one of the most venomous snakes on the planet! The single bite of a king cobra is so strong it could kill an elephant! Luckily, cobras only attack when they feel threatened.

Coyote

These wild dogs are currently thriving throughout North America and down into Mexico and Central America. Coyotes are excellent hunters and eat just about anything, including insects, snakes, fruit, grass, frogs, rabbits, and rodents. They can even take down a deer if they are hunting in packs. Coyotes live in strong family groups. A mating pair of coyotes stays together for several years. In spring, female coyotes give birth to litters of three to twelve pups. Male pups head out on their own when they're six to nine months old, but females usually stay with the parents and become part of the pack.

Cricket

There are hundreds of different species of crickets, and each species has its own distinct chirp! Only male crickets chirp. Their wings have ridges, like the teeth of a comb, that they rub with a hind leg to make a chirping sound. There are two types of chirps. The first alerts and attracts females. The second type of chirp is a softer song meant to woo the females. Crickets are able to hear through ears that are located just below the joint of their front legs. Even though crickets have thin, delicate wings, most varieties cannot fly. If crickets get too hungry, they eat each other!

FUN FACT

Temperature can be measured in cricket chirps! The faster the chirps, the hotter it is. To figure out the approximate temperature outside, add **40** degrees Fahrenheit to the number of cricket chirps you count in **15** seconds.

FUN FACT

Coyotes communicate with other coyotes. Once one coyote calls out, other coyotes join in, creating a loud chorus of howls!

D

FUN FACT

Cellar spiders eat black widow spiders, which are highly poisonous!

Daddy Longlegs

There are two different types of bugs that go by the name of daddy longlegs! Both types have long, thin legs. But one is a spider and the other is not. Their real names are cellar spider and harvestman.

You can tell the two apart because cellar spiders have two body parts and harvestman has only one. And, they see things a bit differently, because the harvestman has two eyes, but cellar spiders have eight! The number of their long, lanky limbs varies as well. Harvestman have six legs, and the cellar spider has eight.

Both types of daddy longlegs are harmless. Cellar spiders are beneficial because they eat other bugs, including other spiders.

Deer

For most species of these majestic animals, only the males grow antlers, but the reindeer is different—both male and female reindeer grow antlers. They grow new antlers each summer, after shedding their old ones the previous winter.

The smallest and most common deer in the United States is the white-tailed deer. These deer are reddish brown and have offspring with spots. One of the largest deer varieties is the reindeer. They live in the far north, where the temperature can get very cold, so reindeer are much more furry than white-tailed deer.

These agile creatures are fast runners and high leapers, so they can stay away from mountain lions, coyotes, and bobcats. They can jump as high as 10 feet and as far as 30 feet in a single bound!

FUN FACT
Reindeer hooves are extra wide and act like snowshoes!

Dolphin

Dolphins breathe through a blowhole on
top of their heads when they surface which
closes up when they dive back underwater.
Some species of dolphins must breathe every
20 to 30 seconds, while others can hold their
breath for as long as 30 minutes!

Dolphins sleep in a most unusual way!
They rest half their brain at a time. While
half of the dolphin brain sleeps, the other
half stays alert with one eye open to watch
for predators.

Dolphins have keen eyesight, but they
also use a type of sonar, called echolocation,
to "see" what is around them.

Donkey

One of the quickest ways to distinguish donkeys from their cousins the horse, zebra, mule, and wild ass, is by their ears. Donkey ears are much longer and have dark markings on them. Donkeys also have white noses and often have white circles around their eyes and white tummies. The mane of a donkey is coarse and stands up straight. The tail is covered with short body hair, with only a tuft of hair at the end.

Donkeys range in size from miniature (under three feet tall) to "mammoth" (about five feet tall), and are measured, like horses, in hands (a hand is four inches).

FUN FACT

A male donkey is called a jack and the females are called jenny or jennet. The babies are called foals, just like baby horses.

Dragonfly

Numbering almost 5000 species, these winged creatures come in a rainbow of colors and have been around since dinosaurs roamed the earth. Fossils of a dinosaur dragonfly have been found with a wingspan of two and a half feet—massive compared to the dragonflies of the world now.

Dragonfly eyes are incredibly complex. They have 30,000 lenses (humans have one) and can see more colors than humans. Humans have three kinds of color receptors in their eyes, which, when combined, make all colors of the rainbow. Dragonflies have four or five different color receptors, so they are able to see additional colors, and can even see ultraviolet light!

FUN FACT

Even though dragonflies have six legs (as all insects do), they cannot walk!

Eagle

There are about 60 species of eagle, and the most common in North America are the bald eagle and the golden eagle. Both have a keen sense of vision, which, paired with sharp talons, makes them excellent hunters. They can see up to seven times farther than humans! Bald eagles make their nests near water and their main food source is fish. Golden eagles live in mountainous areas, grasslands, or prairies and feed on birds and mammals such as rabbits, ground squirrels, skunks, and even foxes and cats!

Because bald eagles are born brown, they are often mistaken for golden eagles, but golden eagles have feathers covering their legs while young bald eagles legs are bare. When they are approximately four years old, bald eagles' head and tail feathers turn white.

FUN FACT

If a bald eagle loses a feather on one wing, a feather will fall out on the other wing, as well, so that it keeps perfect balance!

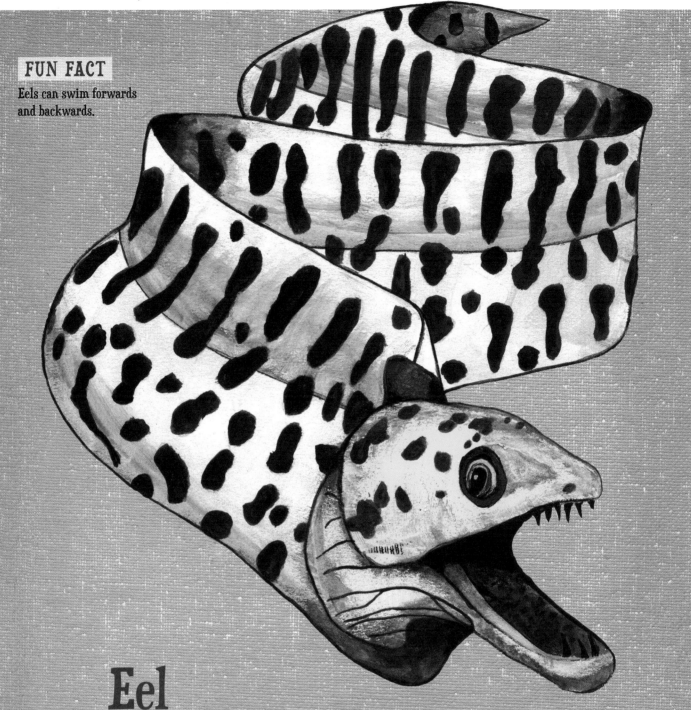

Eel

Even though eels are technically fish, most varieties have skin rather
than scales, covered with a slimy protective coating. These long, snake-
like fish hide in crevices and caves during the day with their heads
peeking out, then prowl for food when the water is dark. Eels come in a
variety of lengths, but moray eels can grow to as long as 10 feet and are
easy to spot because of their bright coloring.

Electric eels are not true eels, but they look similar! Electric eels do
in fact carry an electrical charge, which they use to zap any predators.
In fact, they can emit a burst of at least 600 volts! That is five times the
power of the current in an average wall socket in the United States!

Elephant

Elephants weigh up to six tons (12,000 pounds) and stand almost 10 feet tall! There are two kinds of elephants: African and Asian. The African elephants are the larger of the two. Asian elephants have smaller, rounder ears.

Elephant trunks are long multipurpose noses that they use for drinking, trumpeting, hugging, and even to pick up items as small as a single leaf.

To cool off in hot weather, elephants fill their trunks with water and then spray their bodies. Then they dust themselves to make a protective coating from the sun's harsh rays. They flap their big, floppy ears to further cool themselves down.

Elephants can eat 300 pounds of food each day and can drink 10 gallons of water at a time. They roam great distances to find enough to fill them up.

They have huge teeth as well as extra-long ivory tusks, which they use as weapons. The tusks continue to grow throughout an elephant's life.

FUN FACT

Baby elephants suck their trunks to sooth themselves, much like human babies suck their thumbs!

Elephant Seal

These enormous creatures get their names because of the long, elephant trunklike snout found on males. Elephant seals come on land to breed but spend the rest of their lives (up to 10 months each year) out at sea, where they feed on fish, squid, and other marine animals. These migratory beasts often swim thousands of miles.

Male elephant seals are very territorial, especially when mating. They mate with a group of up to 50 female elephant seals. This group of females is called a harem. When male elephant seals challenge each other over females, they inflate their snouts, roar, and sometimes fight.

FUN FACT

While seal pups are still nursing, mama seals do not eat! They live off of their extra stored-up blubber.

Emu

These huge Australian birds do not fly. Instead, emus are running birds, with long and very powerful legs to run fast. These big birds are also amazing jumpers—they can reach up to seven feet in a single leap.

Emus don't sing or chirp like most birds. They inflate a pouch in their throat and let out a loud sound, similar to drumming or booming, during courtship. They also grunt and hiss when they are warning off predators.

Emus eat almost anything including rocks, dirt, and even cans!

F

Falcon

There are many species of falcon, but the most common, called peregrine falcons, are the fastest birds on earth! These amazing birds of prey hunt other birds among other animals. They fly directly above them and then swoop down to capture them in midair. Falcons can dive through the air at speeds of more than 200 miles per hour!

Falcons travel great distances. They often spend the winter thousands of miles from where they spend the summer. The greatest recorded distance a falcon has flown in one year is 15,500 miles! But when it's time to mate, falcons return to the place where they were hatched.

FUN FACT

Falcons even live in cities, where they build nests on tall buildings and feed on pigeons!

Firefly

These luminous, winged insects,
also called lightening bugs, flash
teeny beams of light to attract
mates. There are approximately
2,000 species of firefly that
can be found zipping through
the night sky in warm, humid
environments. Each of the
species has a distinct pattern
to their flashes, so that potential
mates can find each other!

Animals that light up are
called bioluminescent. There
are several different ways that
animals are able to light up.
Fireflies are able to glow because
they have light organs located
under their abdomens.

The fireflies' blinking light
serves as a warning to predators.

Flamingo

These lanky, long-legged birds
are not naturally pink! Baby flamingos are born gray and white.
Once flamingos reach adulthood,
their feathers turn pink due to
their diet of rose-colored brine
shrimp, which are abundant in the
flamingo's shallow water habitat.
They use long legs to stir the mud,
which they slurp up. Their curved
bills have a built-in filter to remove
the food from the muddy water.

Flamingos spend most of their
time standing around in large
groups called flocks or colonies.
At 10 days old, baby flamingos
join with other new chicks to form
a group or crèche (like flamingo
nursery school) where they are
looked after by adult flamingos.

FUN FACT

The eye of a flamingo is
larger than its brain!

Flying Squirrel

These nimble creatures live most of their lives atop trees, and when they want to move from one tree to the other, flying squirrels spread out their arms and ride the air from branch to branch!

Their unique body has fur-covered skin that spreads out like a parachute from wrists to ankles, allowing them to trap a pocket of air or wind and soar through the air. They also have a flat, furry tail that they use like a boat's rudder to steer them as they glide from treetops to lower branches.

When a flying squirrel sees a predator, its main defense is to stay completely still, so the predator will think it is a a branch, rather than a snack.

Fox

Foxes are often called sly or cunning—and for good reason: Foxes are one of the most adaptable creatures on earth. Foxes can be found all over the world, living in diverse habitats, from snow covered mountains, arid deserts, forests, and grasslands.

There are several species of foxes, including the silver fox and kit fox, but the most common and recognizable is the red fox, with its reddish-brown fur and distinct white-tipped tail.

Foxes have beautiful, thick tails. When it's cold, they wrap their warm tails around themselves when they sleep.

FUN FACT

Arctic foxes turn white in the winter and then back to light brown when the snow melts.

Frog

FUN FACT

The difference between frogs and toads is that toads tend to live on land and have bumpier, dryer skin and walk on stubby legs rather than hop on long ones!

These hopping croakers come in lots of sizes, shapes, and colors! Frogs are all amphibians, which means they are all cold-blooded critters. They have bulging eyes and long, strong legs with webbed feet to help them swim and leap. Frogs can hop up to 20 times their body length!

Frogs hatch from eggs and begin their life cycle starting with the tadpole stage. Unlike adult frogs, tadpoles have gills and live in water. Tadpoles begin to sprout arms and legs then become a froglet, with only a tiny tail stub left, and then finally, they become full-grown frogs.

Frogs begin to croak once they reach adulthood. In most frog species only the males croak to attract female frogs and to warn away other male frogs from their territory.

Gecko

These climbers are able scurry up just about any surface. Their feet are specially equipped with sticky toe pads.

These nocturnal animals have long tongues, which they use to wipe dust and debris off of their eyeballs!

A gecko's tail is detachable. If one of these wily creatures' tail is grabbed by a predator, the gecko can detach it from its body. The separated tail will then wiggle around to distract their attacker. This surprise gives the gecko time to dash away without being caught. A new tail will grow back in a few months.

Giraffe

These gangly leaf-munchers are the giants of the African savanna. The giraffe is the tallest animal on earth—a necessary trait as they forage for leaves at the tops of trees. A giraffe's tongue is 18 to 20 inches long and blue-black. Some scientists believe the dark color is an adaptation to keep the tongue from getting sunburned. Giraffes are approximately six feet tall when they are born and grow to around 18 feet tall! And, no two giraffes have the same pattern of spots. Amazingly enough, even though their necks are so long, giraffes have the same number of vertebrae in their necks as we do—seven. Each one is just bigger than ours!

FUN FACT

The tallest giraffe ever recorded was 29 feet! More than 10 feet taller than most giraffes.

Goldfish

Most of us know goldfish as small pets that swim around in tanks, but they can live for up to 20 years, grow to more than 16 inches, and weigh more than 6 pounds!

Although the name "goldfish" makes it seem that all of these swimmers are orange, there are actually more than 100 varieties of goldfish in shades of gold and silver.

Remarkably, goldfish have teeth in their throats! That means that they can eat (and even chew) plants, algae, insects, smaller fish, and small water creatures.

Goldfish live in schools in the wild and reach adulthood at two years. They breed quickly: Female goldfish can produce thousands of baby goldfish during her life!

Goose

There are several species of these large, honking birds, but the most common goose seen in North America is the Canadian goose.

These large birds are often seen during migration, flapping through the sky in a V formation. Each goose takes a turn leading the group and then gradually moving to the back. The lead goose blocks the wind, which makes flying for the rest of the flock easier. When migrating, geese can fly as many as 1,500 miles in one day!

When baby geese, called goslings, hatch they imprint or form a strong attachment to the first large animal they see. Some goslings have been known to imprint on other animal species, even humans!

Groundhog

These furry rodents chow down all spring and summer to get as chubby as possible because when the first frost comes, they snuggle into their burrows and live off their stored-up body fat until spring.

Groundhogs are excellent diggers. They create extensive burrows and tunnels—as far as five feet underground and 45 feet long! They are mostly herbivores, which means they feed on plants (although they have occasionally been known to snack on a snail or two). If they sneak into a vegetable garden, they can demolish it quickly!

Groundhogs are noisy critters. They make whistling sounds, squeal, grind and chatter their teeth, and even bark when they feel threatened.

FUN FACT

Geese eat a *lot*! They spend around 12 hours each day nibbling on food.

H

Hawk

There are many species of these keen-eyed birds of prey, but the most common in North America is the red-tailed hawk. You can spot these large birds by their distinct coloring: a rich, brown body and the red tail that earned these predators their name.

All hawks have incredibly sharp vision to spot prey even while flying 100 feet above the ground. A hawk's eyes can adjust quickly, allowing it to keep its prey in focus while diving through the air at 120 miles per hour!

Hippopotamus

To keep cool and out of the hot African sun, hippos spend as many as 16 hours a day in rivers and lakes. This is why they're called river horses—which is the translation of *hippopotamus* from Greek.

Hippopotamuses have eyes and nostrils positioned high on their heads so they can see and breathe while mostly submerged. Hippos can also close their nostrils when they go underwater. When they emerge from their swimming holes, they begin to secrete an oily red substance, which may look as if they are sweating blood, but really the red liquid acts as a skin moisturizer and sunscreen.

Hippos can grow up to 12 feet long and weigh between 5,000 and 8,000 pounds! Hippos are fierce when they need to protect their young and give an ear-splitting bellow, much like the roar of a lion.

FUN FACT

These big mouths have the widest jaw of any land animal at two feet across!

Hummingbird

Unlike other birds, hummingbirds can rotate their wings in a circle, allowing them to fly forward and backwards, up, down, or hover in one spot. They can even fly upside down!

During normal flight, their wings beat 60 to 80 times per second, but when excited, they can beat them up to 200 times per second. The quick motion of the wings makes a humming sound, which is how they earned their name. These feisty, little birds are super fast and have been clocked at speeds of more than 50 miles an hour.

Hummingbirds eat five to eight times every hour and consume as much as three times their body weight each day. They use their long beaks and grooved tongues to drink nectar from flowers.

Humpback Whale

These ocean beasts weigh up to 40 tons (80,000 pounds!) and reach up to 50 feet long when fully grown. These huge animals eat tiny krill, plankton, and small fish—but lots and lots of them!

Humpbacks migrate thousands of miles each year, from icy-cold, polar feeding grounds in summer to warm, tropical waters for breeding in winter. They often travel or hunt in groups called pods, containing as many as 200 whales!

Humpbacks communicate with other whales by singing songs that can travel through the water for up to 20 miles and can often last for hours.

Humpback whales have a distinct tail fin, or fluke. They use their fluke to propel themselves out of the water and to make a tremendous splash—called a breach. Sometimes they add a twist and a fin slap as well! Scientists are not sure whether they do this to clear barnacles off of their skin or just for fun!

FUN FACT

Newborn humpbacks drink approximately **100** pounds of their mother's milk a day!

Hyena

Spotted hyenas make a high-pitched chortle that sounds like a laugh, which is why they are known as "the laughing hyena." There are three types of hyenas: spotted, striped, and brown hyenas—the spotted being the largest.

These wily beasts get most of their meals by scavenging, which means that they eat the leftovers of other predators, but they are excellent hunters, too. Hyenas live in large groups called clans. They work together to take down animals, such as antelope or wildebeest. Once they have caught their prey, hyenas often fight over who gets to eat first. Female hyenas are the leaders in the groups (and larger), so they often win. Hyenas eat every bit of their food, including the bones.

FUN FACT

Even though hyenas look a lot like dogs, they are more closely related to cats.

FUN FACT
Like geese, ibis fly
in a V formation.

Ibis

This long-billed shore bird comes in spectacular colors—from brown with purple highlights and a green tail to snowy white to green and bright scarlet! There are many varieties of ibis, and they live in shallow waters in many countries. They use their long, curved bill to dig around in the mud and shallow water to snap up prey. When they locate tasty earthworms, snails, small fish, or frogs, they snap their bill shut and gobble them down.

Ibis live in large flocks, often among similarly tall shore birds such as herons or egrets, who can warn against common predators, including falcons and hawks.

Iguana

There are many species of these huge lizards: including the spiny-tailed (or black) iguana, the banded iguana, the marine iguana, the desert iguana, and the green (or common) iguana. Green iguana are among the largest lizards in the Americas, and can grow to more than six feet in length!

FUN FACT
Iguanas have a spot on their
heads that allows them to
sense light.

Some iguanas live on land, and others spend their time in trees. They are fast and agile critters. They have strong jaws and razor-sharp teeth, as well as sharp tails, which they use like a whip to fend off predators. Like geckos, an iguana's tail can detach if caught, which confuses their predators (who are left with a mouth full of twitching tail) and allows them time to escape.

Impala

When fleeing a predator, these deerlike jumpers can leap distances up to 30 feet—that's about the width of a two-lane road. The graceful impala is a medium-sized antelope that lives in large herds numbering in the hundreds. When a member of the herd sees a hunter it sounds the alarm, and the herd flees together. Impala males have long, spiral horns; the females have no horns at all. When it's mating time, males will clash their horns against each other.

Inchworm

Despite their name, these little green critters are not worms at all. They are a variety of caterpillar on their way to becoming moths. However, inchworms differ from other caterpillars in that their legs are located only at the front and the rear of their bodies, with none in between! Inchworms move by walking their hind legs forward while holding the front legs in place. Then they move the front legs forward while holding the back legs in place. Their middle section arches and straightens out as they scoot along.

If threatened by a predator, they will generate a silk thread and dangle from a leaf until the danger is gone.

Jackal

There are several different species of jackals found in Africa, India, and Asia. Jackals are members of the dog family and do resemble their furry domestic cousins. These wild dogs are generally scavengers, but they also hunt and kill their own prey.

Jackals mate for life and work together with their mate to hunt, raise pups, and protect their territory from other jackals. Both parents raise the pups. In fact, jackal dads are especially "paws on." When it comes to feeding the kids, these extraordinary dads literally give the pups the food from their mouths. They "regurgitate" (bring up partially digested food) and feed it to their pups.

J

FUN FACT

Side-striped jackals can hoot like owls!

Jaguar

These huge, wild cats are the largest of the big cats found in South and Central America. Spotted jaguars are often mistaken for leopards, because they both have light coloring with black spots. However, jaguars have shorter tails and larger heads than leopards, and their spots are different too. Jaguars have spots within their spots—leopards don't. Along the same lines, black-coated jaguars are sometimes thought to be black panthers.

Black jaguars actually have spots, too, but their background coat is so dark, it's hard to tell unless you are very close.

Another thing that distinguishes jaguars from other cats is that they catch fish, turtles, and other tasty treats by jumping right into the rivers of the Amazon.

FUN FACT

Jaguars are so powerful that their only natural enemies are humans and anacondas!

Jaguarundi

These wild cats are not much bigger than house cats. In fact, the tip of its nose to the tip of its tail measures from three to four and a half feet long—half of that being the length of its long tail!

Native to Central and South America, jaguarundi can also occasionally be found in Texas, New Mexico, and Arizona. Jaguarundi cats also have small ears like an otter that earned them the nickname "otter cat." In spite of their small size, they are powerful and excellent hunters, climbers, and swimmers.

Jaguarundi kittens are born with spots that fade as they grow.

FUN FACT
Unlike most cats, jaguarundi also eat fruit!

Jaybird

These medium-sized boisterous birds are very noisy and tend to hop around. There are many species of jays in lots of different colors. Unlike most birds, they bury food—especially acorns and other nuts—to eat later. Jays also eat fruit, worms, snails, eggs, hatchlings of other birds, and even small mice!

Many jaybirds have feathers on their heads called crests. The position of the crest is one way that jaybirds can tell other birds how they feel. When jays are relaxed their crests are down and smooth. But if they are angry or fighting off predators their crests stand straight up!

FUN FACT

Jaybirds bury more acorns than they can eat, and the leftover buried nuts are responsible for the growth of many oak trees!

Jellyfish

Found in oceans throughout the world, jellyfish have no brain, bones, teeth, or blood, and they cannot swim! Their bodies expand, filling with water, and then they contract to squeeze the water out, which jets them along. However, jellyfish are not able to steer!

Most jellyfish are transparent, which makes them invisible to predators. If they need to, jellyfish can fend off predators with their stinging tentacles. Each tentacle has stinging cells that can inject poison. The stings of jellyfish can be deadly.

There are many species of jellyfish. Some are tiny, while others have tentacles up to 120 feet long!

FUN FACT

Jellyfish are not actually fish, which is why they are also called sea jellies.

K

Kangaroo

These fast jumpers are the largest marsupials
in the world! But they don't start out big:
Kangaroo babies, or joeys, are teeny, hairless,
and blind at birth. Once they have grown large
enough, their heads and feet can often be
seen sticking out of the pouch of kangaroo
moms.

Kangaroos live in groups, called mobs.
The male kangaroos are larger, but the females
are faster. The strongest male is the leader
of the mob.

Kangaroos can boing along at a quick
pace—up to 35 miles per hour! They can leap
25 feet in a single jump and reach heights of
6 feet, using their powerful tails as well as
their back legs.

Killer Whale

Killer whales, also called orcas, are actually not whales at all—they are the largest member of the dolphin family!

These beautiful black-and-white sea creatures are serious hunters and make sounds that travel through the water, bounce off other animals which tells them the size, shape, and location of their their prey.

Orcas feast on large marine animals, such as sea lions and other whales, as well as fish and squid. They even eat sea birds and can break Arctic ice to make penguins and seals into lunch.

Killer whales hunt and live together in pods. They communicate with each other by making clicking sounds and whistles.

Koala

These slow-moving animals feed on eucalyptus leaves which are full of poison that would kill other animals, but koalas have bacteria in their stomachs that break down the poison, so they don't get sick.

Like kangaroos, they are marsupials, meaning the females carry their babies, or joeys, in their pouches while they finish developing.

Koala's sleep for up to 18 hours a day! They live in tree branches and snooze away the day, and then wake up at night.

They are excellent climbers because they have two "thumbs" on each of their front hands, and their hands and feet are equipped with long claws that help them scamper easily into the high branches.

FUN FACT
Koala pouches are not upward facing pouches, like the pouches on kangaroos. The opening for koalas faces the back legs.

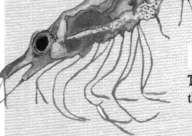

FUN FACT
There are more krill in the world than people!

Krill

Krill is the name for many species of teeny ocean crustaceans and is one of the most plentiful kinds of animal on earth! Scientists estimate that there are millions, and maybe even billions, of tons of krill in the southern oceans. There are hundreds of ocean creatures that depend on the nutritious krill to stay alive. The largest creatures on earth, blue whales, gobble up tons of krill. Seals, whales, seabirds, fish, and squid eat krill, too. Krill live in huge groups, or swarms. They pack together making the water look red or orange. In fact, at certain times of the year, the Antarctic ocean waters are so packed with krill, they can be seen from space!

Ladybug

These little beetles are beloved because of their brightly colored wings and they eat aphids—a common garden pest. Ladybugs can eat as many as 25 to 50 aphids and other plant-eating bugs each day! Most ladybugs have shells that are red with black spots, but there are variations in color and pattern among the different species of ladybugs. All ladybugs begin blue with orange stripes and then shed their shells as they grow, until they transform into their final color.

They don't survive the cold, so ladybugs hibernate! They spend the winter underground in groups and then emerge again in the spring to lay thousands of eggs in aphid-infested areas. That way, when the babies hatch, they have a food source nearby.

FUN FACT

Ladybugs have been into outer space! In 1999, NASA brought four ladybugs on the space shuttle, along with aphids, to see if they could still hunt and eat in zero gravity. They could! Ladybugs do very well in space!

Leafy Sea Dragon

True to its name, this unusual creature looks like a mythical dragon! This perfectly camouflaged fish is related to sea horses and finds its home among leafy seaweed and sea grass in the waters of Australia.

The lobes of skin that grow on the leafy sea dragon's body are not used for swimming. Instead, sea dragons propel themselves along using the transparent pectoral fins on their necks and dorsal fins near their tails. Sea dragons use their long nose to help them steer. Unlike sea horses, they are not able to curl their tails around seaweed or other stationary objects to hold themselves in place. The leafy sea dragon eats mostly plankton and small crustaceans.

Infant sea dragons are independent and ready to live on their own right away!

Lemur

There are many species of these leaping primates, but they all live on the African island of Madagascar and on the tiny islands nearby. Lemurs come in a large variety of sizes and colors. The most commonly recognized is the ring-tailed lemur.

Depending on the species, lemurs make different sounds and eat a range of foods. Many lemurs are herbivores, and like to eat fruit, leaves, bark, and other types of plants. Other lemurs are omnivores and eat insects and eggs, as well as plants.

Lemurs use both their hands and feet to climb trees, and none can grip with their tails. They have strong legs that they use to leap from tree to tree or hop along the ground.

FUN FACT

When lemurs fight, it is usually the females, not the males, who duke it out.

Leopard

These powerful spotted cats can haul large prey high up into the branches of trees to eat. Leopards also use trees as perches, where they hide and then spring down on unsuspecting prey.

Leopards like the water. Not only do they dip in to stay cool during the heat of the day, but they also hunt for fish. Although they love to swim, these amazingly adaptable cats can live without drinking water! They absorb the moisture they need from the food they eat.

Leopards are extremely fast runners and can reach speeds up to 35 miles per hour. They can jump 10 feet straight up and bound 20 feet forward in one leap! Their spotted fur is covered in markings called rosettes, because they look like a rose.

Lion

These massive cats are known as kings for good reason! Male lions are the protectors of their group, or pride, while female lions, which are lighter and faster, are the hunters. Not only do females hunt as a team, they also work together to raise the cubs. Females in the group usually stay together their entire lives.

A new male lion must fight his way into a new pride. Lion manes protect them from the claws of other male lions during battle. If the newcomer loses the fight, he will be driven away by the other males. But if he wins, he will join the pride and may eventually take it over by driving off the older male leader.

FUN FACT

Like many house cats,
lions sleep for up to
21 hours each day!

Llama

These gentle animals are in the camel family, but unlike camels, they do not have humps. Llamas have been domesticated, which means that they no longer live in the wild.

Llamas are very sociable. Babies, called crias, need to stay with their mothers for six to eight months. If they separate from their mother too early, they will imprint on their human caretaker.

These big, fuzzy, two-toed beasts are also excellent pack animals, although they can't carry as much as horses, donkeys, or camels. If llamas get packed with too much weight, they will just lie down.

Lovebird

These darling, brightly-colored birds are actually small, stocky members of the parrot family. Like all parrots, lovebirds have the ability to vocalize and mimic human voices and words, but they are not nearly as talkative as large parrots or macaws. There are nine species of lovebirds, but the two most common are the peach-faced lovebird and the black-masked lovebird. Eight of the nine species of these energetic birds come from Africa; the ninth comes from the island of Madagascar.

They are very social and boisterous birds and live in groups.

Manatee

Sweet, gentle manatees were sometimes mistaken for mermaids in ancient sailing days. Fully grown, these beasts weigh between 750 and 2,000 pounds. It takes at least 100 pounds of food each day to feed these hungry giants!

Manatees have flexible front limbs to both hold their food and steer as they swim. They also have a large, powerful tail to propel them along.

Manatees communicate with other manatees by clicking and chirping. Communication is especially strong between the mother, called a cow, and her baby, called a calf.

M

FUN FACT

Manatees are considered a pest in Africa, because they swim into rice fields and munch on the crop.

Meerkat

These sociable sunbathers are perfectly adapted to keep their bodies the ideal temperature—even in the extreme heat of the African day. They have "sunglasses" in the form of black fur around their eyes, which helps keep down the glare of the bright sun. Their tummies are lightly covered in dark fur, which they turn toward the sun to capture heat. As the day warms up, they stay cool by turning their light-colored furry backs to the hot sun's rays.

Meerkats live in large social groups and make their homes in burrows with sleeping areas. Special earflaps cover their ears to keep out flying dirt. They also have special lenses that cover their eyes, to protect them from dust and soil.

FUN FACT

Unlike most animals, meerkat pups can nurse while their mother is standing up!

Monkey

Monkeys come in many shapes, sizes, and colors, but they all love to "monkey around." Monkeys are divided into two main groups: Old World monkeys, which live in Africa and Asia; and New World monkeys, which live in Mexico and Central and South America. The noses of the two types are different: Old World monkeys have their nostrils set close together, while New World monkeys' nostrils are set far apart. Old World monkeys have pads on their rumps to make sitting easier, but New World monkeys don't spend much time sitting around at all! Instead they use their tails to help them climb trees, where they hang out and play. Old World monkeys do not swing from tree to tree because they don't have tails that can grip onto branches!

Moose

Moose look docile but they are quite fierce! They have long legs and powerful hooves that they use to kick off entire packs of wolves and even bears! A moose's front hooves also work as snowshoes during the extremely snowy, icy winters in Canada and Alaska, where they live. During these freezing months, moose scrape away the ice that covers trees and shrubs and munch on twigs and leaves.

In the summer, moose keep cool and feed on water plants in lakes, marshes, and streams. In fact, some baby moose are able to swim when they are only days old!

Moose are usually quiet animals, but during mating season males and females call to each other with loud bellows.

FUN FACT

Within days of being born, moose calves can run faster than grown people.

Mountain Lion

These majestic cats are also known as pumas, panthers, and cougars. Mountain lions can be found in North, Central, and South America, so they have been named by different groups of people. These powerful felines are very adaptable and can live in different habitats: high in the mountains at 10,000 feet or down at sea level, as well as in deserts, forests, wetlands, and grasslands.

Each mountain lion's territory covers between 30 to 125 square miles! Males span larger areas than females, but males and females don't mind overlapping.

They are powerful, with muscular back legs, large paws, and sharp claws! They can jump as high as 18 to 20 feet in one bound! That is higher than a single-story house!

FUN FACT

Like cheetahs, mountain lions have a flexible spine to help them run fast!

Mouse

FUN FACT

Mice are very organized. Their homes have kitchens, bedrooms, and bathrooms.

These little creatures are big eaters! Mice eat 15 to 20 times a day, sleep in nests that they build in quiet, tucked away places, and are nocturnal, and forage for food at night.

A female mouse is called a doe and a male mouse is called a buck. A baby mouse is either a pinky or a kitten. Mice reach maturity after two months and then they are ready have pinkies of their own. In fact, mice can have up to 100 pinkies each year!

Naked Mole Rat

Hairless, pink, and wrinkly, with long sharp teeth, the naked mole rat is neither a mole nor a rat, and it is not completely naked! Naked mole rats live in the deserts in East Africa, where they are called sand puppies. These sand puppies live almost entirely underground to keep cool during the scorching days. Because of this, they don't need or have much hair. And, because it is completely dark in the tunnels, they are almost entirely blind.

These small critters live in groups called colonies. Every mole rat has a specific job. And, like a bee colony, there is a queen. The queen is in charge of the colony and births all the babies—up to 25 pups in each litter. The queen is not born a queen. She has to fight to gain her place.

FUN FACT

They only have about **100** hairs on their entire bodies, which are more like whiskers that they use to navigate in the deep tunnels underground.

Needlefish

FUN FACT

Needlefish are related to flying fish and, like flying fish, they enjoy jumping out of the water.

As you would guess from their name, needlefish are long, slender, and covered in silver scales. They can be found just under the water's surface in warm seas, near reefs, and in some freshwater rivers and streams. They have distinct long, narrow jaws and teeth, and they hunt by passing prey then turning to snatch the unsuspecting target and swallow it whole. These shimmery predators like to snack on small fish, plankton, and crustaceans.

Needlefish can grow up to four feet long. Their long jaws are filled with sharp teeth that form a spear. Not only can they pierce through waves, they've been known to poke through the hulls of canoes!

Newt

Though a newt might look like a lizard, they are not closely related. A lizard is a reptile that lives on land, whereas newts are amphibians born in the water. These amphibians can regrow not only their tails, but also their eyes, hearts, arms, and legs!

Like frogs, they hatch from eggs, become tadpoles, and grow into adults. Once newts are fully developed, some, but not all, leave the water and live on land. But, they still need to stay cool and moist.

Newts move at a slow pace, which makes them prime targets for predators, but they have adapted to solve that problem—they taste horrible and many are poisonous, so predators keep away!

FUN FACT

Even newts without gills can "breathe" underwater by getting oxygen through their skin.

Nightingale

Nightingales are one of the only birds to sing at night, which is how they earned their name. Like crickets, only the male nightingales twitter the night away in hopes of attracting a mate. The male bird will create a wide variety of sounds from trills and chortles to long extended whistles. These little birds are amazing flyers, traveling long distances from Asia and Europe to Africa, where they live in the winter. In the spring, they return to build their nests and raise their chicks. Nightingales are surprisingly difficult to spot because they blend in to their surroundings.

Nudibranch

Nudibranchs, also called sea slugs, are like colorful confetti on reef walls. They come in a rainbow of colors, including vivid blues, pinks, and oranges—some with spots and stripes. Sea slugs come in a vast array of body shapes and sizes, too. Some of the smallest nudibranch are less than one inch long, while others grow to as much as a foot in length. The word *nudibranch* is Latin and means naked gills because of the exposed gills on the back of many species.

Nudibranchs are meat eaters and feed on mollusk eggs, sponges, jellyfish, anemones, and even corals. Without hard shells, nudibranchs have developed other ways to protect themselves: Some produce a chemical so they taste bad to large hungry fish, while others store stinging cells from the food they eat to discharge when attacked!

Nutcracker

These mountain birds have long, pointy bills that they use to crack open pinecones and nuts (hence their name). They also have a special pouch under their tongues, which they use to store food (like squirrels) until they have time to bury them.

Male nutcrackers are helpful fathers. Along with their mates, they sit on the eggs to hatch them. Male nutcrackers have "brood pouches" to store eggs to keep them warm, just like females. When they hatch, baby nutcrackers, or nestlings, are fed pine seeds from their parents' store of nuts and seeds.

FUN FACT

Nutcrackers can hold between 20 and 90 seeds (depending on the size) in the pouches under their tongues!

FUN FACT

Like garden snails, nudibranch leave a trail of slime behind them.

O

Octopus

With its boneless body, big bulbous head, and eight flowing arms, the octopus is a master escape artist. Octopuses can change to match the colors, patterns, and textures of any undersea environment. It can squeeze through small crevices and hide in hollow shells, and will squirt out a cloud of black ink to hide to cover its trail. If they do get caught, octopuses can lose an arm to avoid a predator's grasp and regrow it later!

In addition to being boneless brainiacs, octopuses have three hearts.

There are about 200 different species of octopuses in many sizes and colors. The giant Pacific octopus is the largest: It can grow to be 30 feet wide and weigh more than 600 pounds!

Orangutan

The largest tree-dwelling animal in the world, these red-haired apes have curved hands and feet. Orangutans have very long arms—twice as long as they are tall—that they use to swing from branch to branch. They build nests each night out of leaves and branches, sometimes as high as 100 feet above the ground!

Orangutans find the water they need in tree hollows, on leaves, or on their own fur after it rains. Some crush up leaves and use them like a sponge to soak up water for drinking.

Orangutans are highly intelligent.

A male orangutan can weigh up to 220 pounds and grow to about four and a half feet tall and are twice as big as females. Orangutans can live up to 40 years in the wild.

FUN FACT

Orangutans communicate through a series of grunts they make using a special throat pouch found right under their chins!

Opossum

These crafty critters are the only marsupial found in North America. When faced with a predator, they fall to the ground with glazed eyes and opened mouth. This is what the term "playing possum" means.

Opossums live in tree holes or in dens made by other animals and have thumbs like humans, so they can hold on to tree branches easily. But unlike people, their thumbs are on their feet! Sharp claws also help their grip, while they use their strong tail to wrap onto the things that they want to hold.

Ostrich

These huge birds are the heaviest and largest in the world. They are also the fastest running bird on earth, reaching speeds of more than 40 miles an hour. Even though they don't use their wings to fly, ostriches use them to balance and steer while they sprint along.

People think ostriches bury their heads in the sand when they are afraid. But they don't. They plop down and press their bodies and necks on the ground to blend in with their sandy environment.

When family groups of ostriches meet, they may challenge each other with short chases, and then the winning adult pair takes all the chicks with them. Some of these "ostrich nurseries" can end up with 300 chicks!

FUN FACT

Unlike other birds, their
feathers have soft edges so
they glide silently through
the sky.

Owl

It is said that owls look wise because of their
huge eyes. In fact, their eyes are so big, they
cannot move them around in the eye socket,
which is why they turn their entire heads
when looking in any direction. (They can
twist their heads three-quarters of the way
around.) Owls also have the best night vision
of any animal.

Owls' ears are almost invisible, but they
have excellent hearing. They are very quiet
when flying, but snort, hiss, screech, whistle,
and clap their wings when trying to impress
a mate.

There are about 200 species of owls. Some
are very small—only four to six inches long
while others have bodies as big as two feet
long, with wingspans of four to five feet wide!

Panda

Most people know the giant panda, with its white-and-black coat. The lesser-known panda, the red panda, is smaller with reddish fur.

Giant pandas live in bamboo forests of China at elevations between 5,000 and 10,000 feet. Bamboo makes up most of their diet. They take 16 hours a day to eat as much as 40 pounds of leaves. When they are not eating, pandas spend their time sleeping.

FUN FACT

While no one knows for sure how the giant panda got his markings, one thought is that the white-and-black fur helps them stand out in the green forests, so they can better find their mates.

Parrot

There are hundreds of parrot species in brilliant colors, ranging from scarlet to vivid green to snowy white. These talkative birds are smart and vocal, and some can imitate human speech. All parrots have four toes on each foot, with two toes pointing forward and two facing backward. This allows them to easily grab onto sticks and branches.

The world's largest parrot is the hyacinth macaw. The heaviest parrot is the kakapo, which weighs up to six and a half pounds and is too heavy for its size to fly. The smallest parrots are the pygmy parrots, which are less than four inches long. Some species of parrots choose a mate for life, and some live as long as 80 years!

FUN FACT

The African gray parrot is one of chattiest birds and has been known to have a vocabulary of up to 700 words!

Peacock

With their bright, shimmery blue heads and their elaborate feathers, peacocks are a very glamorous pheasant. Only the male is truly a peacock. The female is a peahen, and the babies are peachicks! All of them together are called peafowl. There are three kinds of peafowl, but the most well-known species is called the Indian peafowl.

The peacock is the colorful one, while peahens are drab, blending in with the landscape to stay safe from predators. When a male peacock wants to court a peahen, he spreads his beautiful feathers into a semicircle that can be up to seven feet wide and three feet tall! Each feather has an ocelli (a pattern that looks like a colorful eye). If the peahen seems interested, the male shakes his feathers causing the ocellus to sparkle.

FUN FACT
Peacocks can pop their tail feathers up and down quickly—almost like an umbrella.

Penguin

The penguin's black-and-white "tuxedo" serves a purpose. Their black feathers blend in with the dark ocean water, while their white tummies blend into the light reflecting off the surface of the water, hiding them from predators on both sides.

Penguins can be found in several climates. Arctic, or cold-climate penguins, have extra feathers on their legs to keep them warm, while penguins that live in hotter climates have bare legs.

Instead of having wings like other birds, penguins have flippers for swimming. Although most penguin dives are shallow and only last for a minute or two, some species have been known to dive up to 1000 feet or more.

FUN FACT

When traveling on ice, Antarctic penguins often "toboggan" on their bellies, using their flippers and feet to slide their bodies forward along the ice.

Piranha

The name piranha means "fish teeth" and these vicious meat-eating fish have lots of them. If a piranha loses a tooth, it grows a new one right away.

Piranhas are freshwater fish that live in the muddy rivers of the Amazon in South America. They have an excellent sense of hearing and their bodies are lined with "sensors" that pick up the vibrations of potential prey.

The most ferocious species is the red piranha. Red piranhas typically feed in groups of 20 and may swarm if they sense blood in the water. They mostly attack other fish or wounded animals that fall into the water.

Not all piranhas are vicious meat eaters. Of the 20 species only a few eat meat. Most are vegetarians who nibble on plants!

FUN FACT

Red piranhas are terrific dads! They make the nest and watch over the eggs until the babies are born.

Platypus

This quirky beaver-tailed mammal looks like a duck but doesn't act like a duck! Like a bird, the platypus hatches from an egg, but like a mammal, the young feed on their mother's milk, which is released through pores in the skin. Grooves on her belly help form pools of milk, where the babies lap it up until they are three to four months.

Platypi live in pairs and nest in burrows near small streams and rivers where they forage for food. When swimming, platypi close their ears and eyes and rely instead on their big, sensitive bill to guide them along. But beware! Male platypi have a spike on their hind foot to prick predators and deliver poisonous venom, like a snake's fang.

FUN FACT

There are three ways to say the plural of platypus: platypuses, platypodes, or platypi.

Polar Bear

Though a polar bear's fur looks white, the individual hairs are actually clear. Polar bears have two coats of fur and a layer of fat to keep them warm in the Arctic winter. They also have fur on the bottom of their paws that stops them from sliding on the ice. And under all that hair, their skin is black to absorb heat from sunlight.

Polar bears are strong swimmers, and their blubber helps them float, while they use their big paws to paddle around.

Polar bears dig snowy holes, or dens, to snooze in through the cold winter months. While they are hibernating, female polar bears give birth to babies. Polar bear cubs are usually about the size of a human hand at birth and can grow to about 1,500 pounds.

FUN FACT

Polar bears have a powerful sense of smell and have been known to sniff out food over great distances—more than 10 miles away! They can even smell food that has been buried in the snow!

Porcupine

These slow-moving waddlers are covered in thousands of long, sharp spikes called quills. These quills are made of keratin, which is similar to what makes up human hair and fingernails, and can be up to one foot long! When frightened, the porcupine's quills stand up to create a protective shield on its back. A porcupine can have as many as 30,000 quills and some porcupines have barbs on the ends.

Prairie Dog

Prairie dogs are not dogs at all. They are actually large ground squirrels that are found on the prairie. They earned the "dog" part of their name because they bark like dogs.

Prairie dogs live in family groups called coteries, in a system of underground burrows called towns. These developments can be very big, stretching for miles and containing tens of thousands of prairie dogs.

When faced with a predator, prairie dog families work together. At the first whiff of danger, the sentinel—or "lookout"—gives a high-pitched warning bark called a chirk, while jumping up and down. When the predator leaves, they jump and yip, arching their backs to indicate that the danger has passed. This is called a jump-yip!

Praying Mantis

There are between 1,700 and 2,000 varieties of these big-armed bugs, ranging in size from teeny-tiny varieties, that are less than one half inch long, to huge ones that are around a foot in length! The mantis can see up to 60 feet, using its compound-lens eyes in addition to its three lesser eyes.

Praying mantises are masters of camouflage and blend into their environments, whether by turning silver grey inside a rock or brilliant green on a leaf's surface, or in the case of the tropical flower mantises, a light shades of pink. Flower mantises, from Africa or the Far East, so closely resemble flowers that insects will often land on them to get nectar, but find themselves devoured by a hungry mantis instead.

FUN FACT

Female mantises eat their mates after mating. Newly hatched mantises, or nymphs, often make their first meal of each other!

Quahog

Quahogs, or hard-shelled clams, have many names based on their size, including littlenecks, cherry stones, and chowders. Quahogs live just below the surface of sand or mud, but they start their lives in the sea.

Female clams can release from 1 million to as many as 24 million eggs at one time, and a single female may release up to 60 million eggs in a season, but only a small number will become fertilized and grow to become adult clams.

Baby clams don't have shells. The naked, young clams float along on the ocean waters until the quahog develops a heavy shell, at which time it will sink to the bottom of the sea. It will then use its muscular foot to move around.

FUN FACT
Quahogs have been known to live as long as **40** years.

Quail

The tiny, twittering quail likes to take dust baths with its flock! Every day the flock, or covey, sits in the dust and wriggles around on their bellies, flapping their wings until the dust rises and covers their bodies! There are several species of quail, each with distinct markings. The California quail can be spotted by the fancy, dangling head plume found in the middle of its forehead.

Quail make sounds including coos and pips, which they use to communicate with and warn each other. Quail don't like to fly. In fact, quail can often be spotted on the ground, running along, pecking at seeds and bugs. When danger approaches, they hide or scoot under brush.

FUN FACT
Quails lay lots of eggs—up to 18 at a time.

Queen Snake

These sleek water snakes smell with their tongues! They make their homes in running streams, where they snack on young crayfish that haven't yet formed hard shells as well as tadpoles, snails, shrimp, and insects. Although queen snakes have small, sharp teeth, and will bite, they are not poisonous or aggressive.

Queen snakes can give birth to as many as 20 babies in less than three seconds! Baby snakes are born with extra stripes that fade as they get older.

Queen snakes hibernate throughout the winter and groups of them can be found intertwined near water. During this time, the snakes are sleepy and slow.

FUN FACT

Queen snakes shed their skin twice in the first week after they are born.

Quetzal

A quetzal is a gorgeous bird with a ruby-red breast, bright green-and-blue feathers, and a white-crested head. With its beautiful, long wing and tail plumage, the quetzal was once considered the "god of the air" by the Mayan people.

Males have yellow beaks and females have black beaks. During the mating season, the male's tail feathers grow extra long—up to two to three feet—to catch the eye of their favorite female. If a male's tail feathers grows so long they can no longer fit into the nest, males sit facing backwards with their tails hanging out. Quetzals have especially large eyes that help them see in the dark jungle.

FUN FACT

The quetzal is the national bird of Guatemala, and their money is named after it.

R

Rabbit

Rabbits and hares are closely related but begin life differently. Rabbits are born helpless and hairless and do not open their eyes until they are two weeks old, whereas hares are born with their eyes open. A baby rabbit is called a bunny, while a baby hare is called a kit.

Both have teeth that never stop growing! Rabbits are nearsighted, and on top of that, they have a blind spot right in front of their faces, which is why they turn their heads to look at you.

When they are excited rabbits might stomp a hind leg or jump as high as three feet in the air and twist in a motion called a binky.

Raccoon

With their dark furry masks, white faces, and fluffy ringtails, raccoons look like furry bandits and have been known to steal bird eggs, poach fish, and pillage urban trash.

These mischievous animals are surprisingly tidy. They wash their food before they eat it by holding the food and plunging it into water.

Raccoons are also agile and can even climb down a tree headfirst using their big claws. They can also shimmy down backwards.

FUN FACT

Racoons have a special set of whiskers on their front paws that are so sensitive they feel things before they actually touch them.

Rattlesnake

Like all venomous snakes, rattlers have poison that can be injected into their victims through their sharp fangs. Their mouths can open 180 degrees to eat animals that are *much* bigger than they are! Rattlesnakes hide while they digest, so they don't get eaten themselves. Rattlesnakes use their tongues as sensors to find food. The fork of the tongue helps them smell. These keen animals also rely on special heat sensors. They have two pits under their nostrils that are used to detect heat, sensing when warm-blooded animals are near, allowing them to hunt day or night.

FUN FACT

Newborn rattler babies don't have rattles, but they are still poisonous when they bite!

Raven

Ravens are the acrobats of the air! They soar, swoop, twirl and loop
upside down. They are incredibly playful and are known to pull pranks,
play tag, and steal food from other animals! Ravens nest all over North
America in desert rocks, forest trees, and the coast.

Sleek with shiny, blue-black feathers, ravens are often mistaken for
crows. The raven is larger and, unlike crows, have wedge-shaped tail
feathers. Ravens can also soar without moving their wings, while
crows need to constantly flap theirs.

Ray

There are more than 500 species of these gliding sea creatures. The two best-known species are the manta ray and the stingray. The manta ray is the largest with a wingspan of up to 25 feet—the length of many swimming pools.

Like sharks, rays do not have bones. Instead their skeletons are made of a hard, rubbery cartilage. They have flat bodies, giant floppy fins, and huge gills. Their eyes are on top of their heads, which allows them to see above when resting or swimming along the sandy bottom of the ocean.

Rays have jaws and their teeth are tough enough to crack the hard shells of clams! Some rays have one to three barbed and poisonous spines at the end of their long tails, but they only sting as a defense. In fact, most rays are very gentle. Rays are also terrific diggers, using their snouts to dig trenches in search of food.

FUN FACT

Electric rays have organs in their fins that generate electrical currents.

Rhinoceros

In Greek, the word *rhino* means "nose" and *ceros* means "horn"—which explains the origins of the name of this famously large-nosed, horned animal.

There are five different species of rhinos. Two of them (Javan and Indian) have only one horn on their heads, while the three others (Sumatran, black, and white) have two horns. Rhino calves are born without horns, which grow in as the baby rhinos grow up.

With massive girth, rhinos weigh up to 5,000 pounds! They have big heads but very small brains and bad eyesight. They have thick skin that is surprisingly sensitive to bug bites, so they roll around in the mud to soothe itchy skin. The mud also serves as a natural sunscreen.

Rhino babies, or calves, weigh up to 150 pounds at birth and drink gallons of milk each day!

FUN FACT

Roadrunner nests often include something very unusual: snakeskin!

FUN FACT

A group of rhinos is called a crash.

Roadrunner

These speedy birds can run up to 20 miles an hour in open chaparral or in the desert where they live. Roadrunners are in the cuckoo family and are also called ground cuckoos.

Speedy movements are key to their survival. Roadrunners are so fast they can catch and eat a coiled rattlesnake before it strikes and have been known to snatch small birds and insects in mid-flight! Because they don't fly, roadrunners build their nests low to the ground in small trees, bushes, or even in cacti.

Roadrunners mate for life and nest only after it rains, because rain means food will be available for their young.

S

FUN FACT

Sea lions groan, honk, roar, and make lots of noise when they are together, but a baby can always hear its mother's call.

Sea Lion

With their big flippers and pointy noses, sea lions and seals look similar. However, sea lions have visible ears, while seals' ears are tiny holes in their heads. Seals and sea lions also "walk" differently on land: Sea lions can twirl their hind flippers in front to wobble around, but seals can only slide and roll to get around.

Both creatures dive deep into the sea to hunt for fish and shellfish. While underwater, they can slow their heartbeat, enabling them to stay under for long periods of time before coming up to breathe.

Sea lions live together in big groups, so there can be up to thousands of sea lions and their pups, together in one spot.

Sea Otter

Sea otters are playful members of the weasel family. They use their strong, flat tails and webbed feet to steer, dive, bounce, and twirl. Especially adapted for the cold ocean, sea otters have two layers of fur—a dense undercoat that traps air and creates insulation, and a second coat that keeps them waterproof.

Sea otters bob on top of the water entwined with seaweed so they don't drift away. They gather mussels, urchins, octopuses, and crustaceans and store their food in a loose pouch of skin. Then they turn on their backs and use rocks to pound open tough shells and pull out the meat with their dexterous paws.

FUN FACT
Sea otters are one of the only animals to use rocks as a tool.

FUN FACT
Some sea stars can grow back their bodies from a lone arm, because most of the sea star's organs are in its limbs.

Sea Star

Sea stars, also known as starfish, are not fish at all. They do not have gills, scales, or fins, and they don't swim. Instead, their tiny tube feet help them move along. Sea stars have bony hard skin, no brains, and no blood!

There are more than 2,000 sea star species that come in all sizes and colors from lavender to white and red. Most sea stars have five arms but some have more. Because a sea star's eyes are at the end of its arms, it can have many eyes, but can't see very well!

Sea stars have a special way to eat. They push their own stomach into the clam or oyster shell and digest it, then bring their stomachs back into their own bodies.

Shark

These predators are known as super hunters for many reasons! Sharks have a keen sense of smell to sniff out prey. They also know when prey is near because they can feel the vibrations of other animals.

Sharks have extremely powerful jaws. Unlike most animals, both the lower and the upper part of the shark's jaws move, which helps them clamp onto their prey, and shake it back and forth to tear loose the meat, which they swallow whole. Sharks also have several rows of razor-sharp teeth that continue to grow throughout their lifetime.

Shark skin is covered with "denticles"— small and very hard scales that are made from the same material as teeth. These hard scales form a type of body armor to protect them—especially from other shark bites!

FUN FACT

Sharks can grow **20,000** teeth in their lifetime!

Skunk

These cute, furry creatures are easy to recognize not only because of their distinct black-and-white or brown-and-cream coloring, but also because they are so stinky! Skunks keep predators away by shooting an oily liquid that smells incredibly horrible. They can shoot the foul-smelling liquid as far as 10 feet!

Although skunk spray is not poisonous, it does keep predators at bay. Owls are the exception because they have hardly any sense of smell. They don't mind if their dinner stinks!

Skunks are nocturnal and eat plants, fruit, eggs, worms, small mammals, fish, snakes, and other small reptiles.

Sloth

Sloths are one of the slowest-moving animals on earth. There are two kinds of sloths: two-toed and three-toed. Both types are about the size of a small dog.

Sloths live in trees hanging upside down! Their long, strong claws help them grip onto branches. Sloths even mate and give birth while hanging in the trees! Their grip is so strong that even a dead sloth will sometimes continue to hang suspended from a branch. On land, sloths are weak and clumsy.

Sloths sleep up to 20 hours every day. Even when awake they often remain motionless so they don't use up a lot of energy. Because of that, these lazy critters don't need to eat much.

FUN FACT

Many land snails are both male and female. Each snail has both eggs and the means to fertilize the eggs, but they need to mate in order to have babies.

Spider

Most people think spiders are insects, but they are not. Spiders are arachnids, as are scorpions, mites, and ticks. What distinguishes arachnids from insects is that they have four pairs of legs and no antennae. Spiders come in lots of shapes and sizes! The largest spider, called the goliath bird-eater, has legs up to 11 inches long and is so large it can eat birds! The smallest spider, called the Patu marplesi, is the size of a typed dot! Think about how small their babies must be!

All spiders spin silk webs. When a spider makes a web, it squeezes the liquid silk out of two small holes at the back of its body called spinnerets. When the liquid silk touches the air, it dries into a thread that the spider then weaves together.

Snail

The snails you see in your garden are just a few species of thousands. Most snails live in the sea or freshwater all over the world. All snails have spiral shaped shells.

Most snails have thousands of teeth on their tongues, which they use to nibble on leaves and other vegetation. Their eyes are at the end of their tentacles and they have no hearing. You may know where a snail has been by the glistening trail it leaves with its "foot," which is really just a big muscle. This silver snail slime allows the snail to create suction allowing the snail to grip onto all kinds of surfaces.

FUN FACT

If you measured it by weight, spider silk is one of the strongest materials on earth.

Swordfish

A swordfish's "sword" is actually a bill, like a bird's beak. Swordfish use their bill to kill their prey but not by spearing. Instead they use their sword like a baseball bat, waving it around to wound surrounding fish.

Swordfish are very fast swimmers. They streak through the water at 60 miles per hour—faster than most cars on the highway!

These big fish can survive in a variety of water temperatures, because they have a unique adaptation that helps them regulate their body heat: They have special tissue near their eyes that keeps their brains warm, so they can survive in frigid water.

FUN FACT

Female swordfish can release more than 25 million eggs in one season!

Tasmanian Devil

T

These fierce animals are marsupials like kangaroos, but are thought of as the hyenas of Australia. Like hyenas, they consume not just the meat of animals, but the hair and the bones, too. Tasmanian devils earned their name because of their devilish behavior: They snarl, bare teeth, growl, and scream. One unusual fighting technique they use is the ferocious sneeze! The devil doesn't use it in an attempt to give their foe a cold, but to make a noise as a challenge, bluff, or scare tactic.

FUN FACT

When Tasmanian devils are about to fight, the tips of their ears turn red and they emit a stinky smell.

Tarantula

Like poisonous snakes, tarantulas inject venom into their prey with fangs. The venom is too weak to cause harm to people, but extremely effective against insects, other spiders, and small animals, such as mice and frogs. Tarantulas don't hang out in webs, waiting for food like other spiders. They live in burrows and come out at night to search for prey. Instead of wrapping their prey in a silken spider's web, they grab it and inject the paralyzing venom with their fangs. Then venom liquefies the prey so that the tarantula can suck up the animal without even chewing!

Tiger

Tigers live alone and leave messages for each other by scratching trees and marking places to claim their hunting territory. Female tigers stay out of other female's territory, and male tigers stay out of other male's territory, but male and female territories overlap so they can mate.

Tigers are fierce hunters that often travel several miles each night in search of prey. When they spy an animal they want to take down, they silently stalk it until they are approximately 30 feet away.

With incredible speed, they run and grab the animal with their huge front paws, biting its neck. Tigers can eat 30 to 40 pounds of meat in one night.

FUN FACT

Tigers are the largest cats in the world.

Toucan

These big-billed birds use their beaks to pluck fruit from hard-to-reach places, including other bird's nests. A toucan's bill can be four times the size of its head.

Toucans also use their unusually large beaks to toss fruit to each other when they're courting.

The beaks may look heavy, but they're constructed similarly to honeycomb and are full of air—making them nice and light!

Toucans live in small flocks of between 6 and 12 birds, and they stick with one mate.

FUN FACT

When toucans sleep, they turn their heads backward and tuck their bills under their wings, then flip their tails over their heads to form a cozy ball of feathers.

Turtle

There are several varieties of these shelled creatures, ranging from teeny-tiny to giant. The smallest turtle is only three to four inches long when it is fully grown. The largest type of turtle grows up to eight feet!

The difference between turtles and tortoises is that turtles live mostly in water, whereas tortoises live on land. Turtles have webbed feet for swimming, but tortoises have round, padded feet for walking on arid land.

A turtle's shell is part of its skeleton. Turtles can feel through their shells, similar to how people can feel through their fingernails.

Turtles have an amazing ability to navigate. Some sea turtles can migrate thousands of miles and still find their way back to the beach where they were born.

FUN FACT

Turtles don't have teeth. Instead they have hard beaks, similar to a bird's.

U

Umbrella Bird

Although these birds live in the tropical rain forest, the feather crest that makes up the "umbrella" on their heads is not used to keep them dry! Instead, the crest, which can face forward or be folded back, is used as an elaborate way to attract a mate. Most umbrella birds also have a long, feather-covered wattle, which hangs below their beak. The bare-necked umbrella bird has a naked, orange-red wattle that is decorated with one single feather at the tip!

During mating season, male umbrella birds form a group, called a lek, where they hang out with inflated wattles to show off for the ladies.

FUN FACT

Like a blow horn, umbrella birds can inflate their waddle with air to make louder bird calls.

Upland Gorilla

This peaceful primate is also known as the mountain gorilla, because it lives high in the rain and bamboo forests and on mountain slopes in Africa. These massive knuckle walkers live in troops of up to 30 gorillas that are led by a strong male gorilla called a silverback. The silverback decides where the troop should go each day and sleep each night. This is no small task, because gorillas never stay in the same place for more than one day. The silverback is also in charge of the safety of the troop. He defends the group from other male gorillas that challenge him; pounding his chest, baring his teeth, screaming, and lunging at his adversary. If that doesn't work, the gorillas will fight—sometimes to the death!

Urchin

Also known as sea urchins, these spiky creatures are covered in movable spines. Some of the spines are solid and others are hollow and filled with poison to keep predators away.

Urchins are found around the rocky shores or coral reefs in the ocean. They come in many sizes and colors, including purple, green, white, brown, red, and black. While they appear to be stuck to rocks or coral, urchins are quite mobile. The ends of their tiny tube feet have little suction cups that they use to grip and movefrom one place to another. They also use their suction-cup-covered feet to pick up rocks and seaweed, which they use to cover their bodies to hide from enemies.

V

Velvet Swimming Crab

Unlike most crabs this feisty crustacean doesn't scoot sideways on its legs. Instead it swims through the water. Velvet swimming crab's pinchers are covered in a soft, reddish-brown fur. Velvet crabs are also known as devil crabs because of their bright red eyes and aggressive behavior.

When they hatch the tiny newborn crabs look more like shrimp than crabs. As they grow they lose and regrow their shell several times before they reach adulthood.

FUN FACT

Vicunas whinny to alert the herd to danger, hum to greet to each other, and say "Gaaaa" when they are angry or looking for a mate.

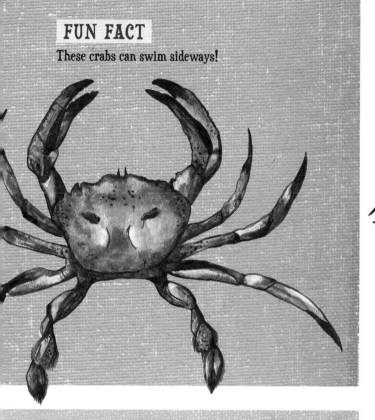

Viper

Vipers are extremely poisonous snakes that have long, hinged fangs and produce venom, which is toxic spit! Sometimes instead of injecting their venom, vipers will bite with dry fangs to give a warning. Their fangs are long and hollow and rotate when they take a bite.

Rattlesnakes, cottonmouths, and adders are all members of the viper family. Like many snakes, vipers can open their mouths very wide (much wider than people and most other animals) so that they can eat big things.

Almost all vipers have keeled scales (a ridged scale, instead of a smooth scale like most snakes) with short tails, and triangular-shaped heads, wide enough to hold their venom glands.

Vicuna

These hearty, grass-eating creatures are the smallest member of the camel family. Even fully grown, they only stand about three feet tall. Vicunas are covered in thick fur, which helps them stay warm in the freezing temperatures of the Andes Mountains, where they live.

Vicunas have padded feet, which allows them to travel over long distances, and their hooves are small and hard so they can climb rocky mountains. Unlike camels, vicuna are not able to survive for long periods without water.

Most vicunas live in groups of about five to twenty females that are led by a single male, while other groups are male-only!

Vole

With stout bodies, long fur, and short tails, voles are often mistaken for field mice, moles, and lemmings. A single female vole can have up to 60 babies a year! Because voles only live to between one month and two years, quick reproduction helps the species survive.

Voles are capable of tunneling up to 15 inches in only one minute! They spend most of their time digging and living in underground burrows that are connected by a system of "secret" runways hidden under brush and ground cover. The voles use these runways to travel from burrow to burrow, only emerging from underground to scavenge edible roots and bulbs.

FUN FACT

Many voles are great swimmers, too!

FUN FACT

Vultures don't make nests and lay their eggs directly on the ground.

Vulture

There are many species of these hunched-looking birds, and they all eat carrion—the remains of decomposing animals. Vultures can be found all over the world, but the most common vulture in North America is called the turkey vulture, because it has a featherless, red head, that looks similar to a turkey's. Turkey vultures can sniff out the scent of dead animals from afar.

Turkey vultures can shoot their vomit up to 10 feet away to fend off predators. Even baby turkey vultures vomit on other animals! They sometimes even throw up on their own food to discourage competing scavengers.

Walrus

These blubbery beasts can grow up to 11 feet long and can weigh more than 3,000 pounds. Their blubber (stored fat) keeps them warm in freezing waters. Walruses are awkward on land but are sleek swimmers in the sea.

Both males (bulls) and females (cows) have tusks that can grow to as long as three feet. Males use their tusks as fierce fighting tools against polar bears and other foe and to protect their harem (female walruses) during mating season. Walruses also use their tusks to drag themselves onto land.

These huge animals feed on small crustaceans, such as clams, sea stars, and other bottom-dwelling critters. To feel their way in the sea's dark depths, they use their long, sensitive whiskers. Walruses can stay underwater for up to 30 minutes at a time.

FUN FACT

The Latin name for walrus translates as "tooth-walking sea horse!"

Warthog

These pigs are not pretty! Warthog faces have several large bumps, which is why the word "wart" became part of their name. But the bumps serve a good purpose—they are actually pads that act as little shields when males battle each other during mating season. These wild swine are smart and adaptable, allowing them to thrive in harsh, dry climates.

Warthogs can survive for months without water. They have large noses and a keen sense of smell to sniff out roots, grasses, tree bark, and berries. Although these tusked swine can be ferocious fighters, they often prefer to flee when danger approaches. They are quite speedy and can run as fast as 30 miles per hour! They hide facing forward in burrows so that they are positioned to attack.

Water Buffalo

Water buffalo horns are almost as long as the animals are tall! Male water buffalos stand between five and six feet tall, and their horns are close to five feet in length. The females also have horns, but they are smaller than the male's.

Water buffalo originally came from Asia and are also called Asian water buffalo, but they have been introduced and domesticated in other countries as well. Both wild and domesticated water buffalo wallow away the day, sunk deep in muddy water. They have wide, hoofed feet, which help to keep them from sinking too deeply in the goo at the bottom of the swamps and marshes where they forage and eat aquatic plants.

FUN FACT

Male water buffalo horns are ridged, but the female's are not.

Whale

There are many species of these majestic sea creatures, and they are divided into two separate categories: toothed whales and baleen whales. Toothed whales have teeth and only one blowhole, while baleen whales have no teeth and two blowholes.

Baleen whales include the three largest species—humpback, gray, and blue whales. Instead of teeth, these whales have baleen in their mouths—similar to a comb covered in fine hair that lets tiny organisms in, but keeps larger stuff out. These whales take in huge amounts of seawater so they can capture the tiny zooplankton, crustaceans, and krill they feed on.

Toothed whales are smaller and eat a larger variety of food, including fish, squid, seals and other small whales. Sperm whales are the largest species of toothed whale.

Toothed whales whistle, moan, and squeal, as well as emit sound waves. Toothed whales use echolocation to navigate when they migrate long distances, which can be as many as 12,000 miles each year!

FUN FACT

The blue whale is the largest living mammal ever—it can grow to **100** feet long!

Weasel

Small and cunning, weasels are in persistent search of food. While they feed mostly on wild mice and small animals, they have been known to sneak into farms to snatch chickens and eggs. The weasel's long, thin body allows it to chase its prey into the narrow tunnels and dens where they live. The weasels then often inhabit these burrows. Weasels are quick diggers, which helps them escape when they are the ones being chased!

Weasels are usually born in the spring, in litters of four to six babies or kits. Kits are born helpless, but they mature quickly and are able to live on their own after only eight weeks.

Whip-poor-will

This North American night-hunting bird strategically resembles a tree branch! Whip-poor-will feathers are medium and dark brown, so when it is sleeping during the day, perched on a tree or among the leaves on the forest floor, other predators never know it is there.

Unlike most birds, whip-poor-wills make their nests on the ground. When it is time to lay eggs, whip-poor-wills lay one or two eggs hidden among the leaves and bushes.

Whip-poor-wills hunt during flight. They gobble up flying insects such as moths, flies, and gnats.

Because they are so well camouflaged, they are rarely seen, but these night birds are especially noisy at dusk, when they call to their mates.

Whooping Crane

These boisterous avians stand five and a half feet, and are the tallest birds in North America. With a population of only 16 birds, whooping cranes were almost extinct until a huge conservation effort saved them.

Whooping cranes mate for life. When they are ready to take a mate, they strut and show off—ruffling their feathers, flapping their wings, and stomping their feet in a mating dance. If another crane is interested, it will mimic the same movements. The two birds will dance side by side, and then show that they are a bonded pair by making birdcalls together.

FUN FACT

Whooping cranes are named for their loud trumpet-like call and the fact that they like to whoop it up, when they are performing the mating dance.

Wolf

Wolves live and hunt in groups called packs. There are two leaders in each pack: the alpha male and the alpha female. They are usually the oldest and strongest in the group and are the only two wolves in the pack to mate.

Wolves have very strong bonds and communicate with each other often. When one of the leaders is alone, he or she can howl to the rest of the pack. Other times the whole pack will howl to let other wolf packs know when they start a hunt. Wolves sometimes howl to show aggression if they are fighting off a predator. Wolves also yip and growl, much like domestic dogs.

FUN FACT

Wolves are strong, fast runners. They can run up to **40** miles per hour and as long as **20** minutes at a time.

Wombat

Just like koala bears and kangaroos, wombats are marsupials that live in Australia and Tasmania. There are two kinds of wombats: the hairy-nosed wombat and the common wombat (although both wombats have hairy noses). Like all marsupials, wombats have pouches to carry their babies.

These fuzzy little animals love to dig! They burrow, making big tunnels up to 100 feet long, which often include a sleeping chamber. Wombats are shy and rarely seen. They spend a lot of time in their tunnels—about three-fourths of their lives they're underground! They are nocturnal, emerging in the evening to feed on grasses, roots, and bark.

Woodpecker

These noisy birds use the hammering sound of their beaks against wood to establish their territories and tell other woodpeckers to stay out! There are more than 200 different kinds of woodpeckers and they all have hard beaks and long pointed tongues that end in a sharp barb. Woodpeckers peck holes and flick their tongues into the holes to spear grub and other insects they uncover.

When it comes to nesting, woodpeckers peck a hole in a tree or branch to create a spacious nest. To make a hole large enough, the process usually takes two to six weeks.

X-Ray Fish

You can see through the transparent skin and scales of this little fish, which is how it earned its name.

X-ray fish like to stay in groups, because they are a "shoaling" fish. Shoaling fish are different than schooling fish, because fish that swim in schools face the same direction but shoaling fish flutter around in different directions within the group.

The body of an X-ray fish is slightly silver or yellow, with a large spot on the fins, a faint yellow stripe along its body, and a reddish tail. These tiny fish usually reach less than two inches in length when fully grown.

Yak

These shaggy beasts are able to live at a higher altitude than any other animal—as high as 20,000 feet! Yaks have enormous lungs, allowing them to breathe more oxygen at higher elevations.

Males can weigh more than 2,000 pounds and stand up to six feet tall. Yak coats have a thick undercoat of fur to keep them warm in freezing cold temperatures.

In addition to their warm coats, their body temperature is higher than most mammals. Both female and male yaks have long, strong horns to dig through the snow and ice to find food underneath.

Female yaks are social animals and stay together in large herds, while male yaks prefer to be alone—except, of course, during mating season.

FUN FACT

When yaks travel through snow, they follow each other single file, all stepping precisely on the footprints of the lead yak.

Yellowlegs

These shy shorebirds live in fresh- and saltwater wetlands, where they feed on small fish and crustaceans.

Yellowlegs fly thousands of miles each year when they migrate! When they arrive at their destination in mid March, it is time to turn around and head back home to make nests and lay eggs. They repeat this cycle throughout their lives.

Unlike most birds, baby yellowlegs can leave the nest shortly after they are born, even before they can fly! Yellowlegs build their nests on the ground, close to the water, so that the chicks can eat and drink all by themselves. But the chicks stay close to their parents, who care for them until they can fly.

Yellow Jacket Wasp

These wasps are often mistaken for bees, because they are a similar size and have the same coloring. But stay clear of them! Unlike honeybees, wasps can sting multiple times. And unlike bees, wasps rely on animal protein for food, which they get from eating other bugs and from food scavenged from the garbage.

Yellowjackets build their nests out of wood that they chew up to form a pulp that dries like mud. The nest, which also looks like dried mud, houses many yellowjackets in a group, called a colony. The colony operates like a beehive, made up of a queen and workers.

Yellowjacket colonies die off over the winter, so the nests are only used for one season.

Yellow-Tailed Black Cockatoo

The largest of the cockatoo species, the yellow-tailed black cockatoo can live to be 100 years old! In the wild, they live in Australia in forests of eucalyptus, pine, or oak in large families.

Both female and male yellow-tailed black cockatoos work together to build nests. There are usually two eggs in the clutch, and of those two eggs, often only one baby chick survives. These cockatoos grow to two feet tall and have black bodies with yellow cheeks.

The bottom of their tail is also filled with yellow feathers, so if you see them flying overhead, the tail looks yellow (hence their name).

FUN FACT

Though rare, there are some yellow-tailed "black" cockatoos that are all yellow.

Yellow Thick-Tailed Scorpion

This fierce animal has an exoskeleton—a skeleton on the outside of its body—eight legs, including two large front legs with pinchers on the end, and a tail that ends in a venom-filled tip. There are about 1400 species of scorpion, but one of the most poisonous is the yellow thick-tailed scorpion.

When hunting, yellow thick-tailed scorpions burrow into loose soil, where they hide to pounce on unsuspecting prey. They grab the prey with their pinchers and shoot poisonous venom from their tail.

Yellow thick-tailed scorpions have multiple sets of eyes: one set on the top, and two sets on each side of their heads.

Zebra

Some scientists believe that zebras are striped to confuse predators, as it is more difficult to pick out any one zebra from a herd during a chase. Each zebra has its own unique pattern. No two zebra's stripes are the same!

Zebra families are made up of a male zebra, called a stallion, and several female zebras, or mares, as well as their babies or foals. The families join together to form a herd. Members of the herd eat together, often groom each other, and defend each other using their powerful back legs. Zebras are fast and run up to 35 miles per hour. Foals are also quick on their hooves. They can walk just minutes after they are born and begin to run about one hour later.

FUN FACT

Zebras "smile" at each other, baring their teeth in greeting, kind of like people!

Zebra Dove

This striped bird's favorite roosting spot is high up in coconut trees. Unlike most birds, zebra doves can produce milk. Crop milk, as it is called, is produced by special glands in both the female and the male birds' gullets (necks), or crops. These glands enlarge and produce a milky substance when they have chicks, so they don't have to be out foraging for extra food when there are extra beaks to feed. Because this gives their babies a better chance of survival, zebra doves lay fewer eggs. They lay one, or at the most two, eggs at a time.

Their zebra-striped feathers help them stay camouflaged when they feed on the ground.

FUN FACT
When zebra dove feathers disintegrate, they form a waterproof powder that keeps them dry.

Zebra Fish

This small freshwater fish has bold stripes on its body, like its mammalian namesake. Like most fish, zebra fish have no eyelids. Their eyes stay moist in the water, so they have no need to blink. Although they don't get any shut-eye, zebra fish do sleep. They stay motionless and rest on the bottom while they snooze.

Zebra fish hatch from eggs that are fertilized by the males after the female has laid them. Brand-new baby zebra fish are called hatchlings. Zebra fish swim in schools.

Zebra Finch

The natural habitat of these beautiful little birds covers most regions of Australia. Most often found in groups, zebra finches are naturally social and get along well with other bird species.

Zebra finches are excellent parents. The mating pair works together to build a nest, and both the male and the female sit on the eggs to keep them warm. The eggs hatch after about two weeks and both parents help to raise the baby chicks.

Each zebra finch's birdsong is unique—just slightly different from every other zebra finch's song! The male birds sing to attract a mate; the female birds rarely sing at all.

FUN FACT
Zebra finches can survive with little to no water!

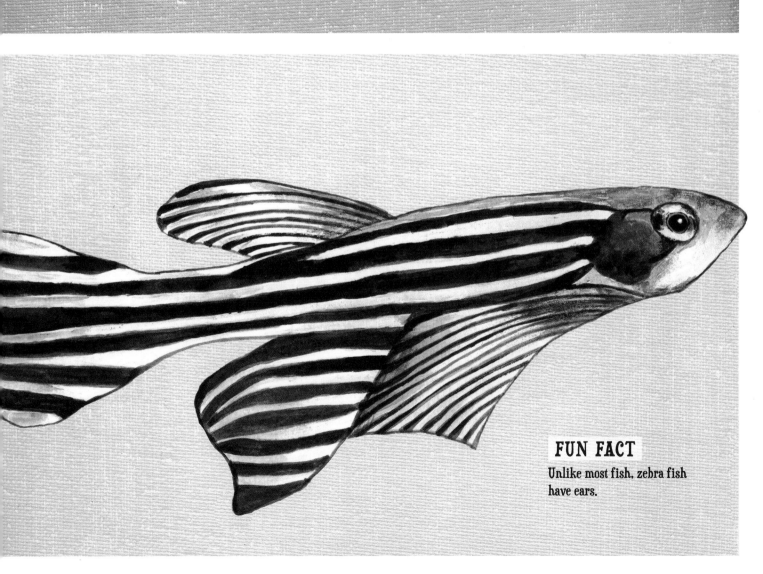

FUN FACT
Unlike most fish, zebra fish have ears.

Zigzag Salamander

There are several species of these unusual amphibians. Zigzag salamanders hatch from eggs, but unlike some salamanders, they do not go through a tadpole stage. Instead, they hatch fully formed. All salamanders need to stay moist and live in wet places, such as leaf litter and the cool crevices of boulders.

Zigzag salamanders come in a variety of colors. Some have zigzagging red stripes while others are brownish-gray. All have long, thin, moist bodies, stubby legs, and a long tail. Like newts, salamanders can regenerate—if a salamander loses a body part, such as a leg, its tail, an eye, or even part of its heart by accident or injury, it will grow back!

FUN FACT

Zigzag salamanders are one of the most common salamanders in the United States.

GLOSSARY OF TERMS

anemones: |a-nem-o-neez| Sea animals of varied colors with clusters of tentacles that resemble a flower.

bioluminescent: |bi-o-lu-mi-nes-ent| An emission of light from living organisms.

carnivore: |kar-ne-vor| An animal that eats other animals.

carrion: |ker-e-on| Decaying dead animals.

echolocation: |eko-lo-kay-shun| A process for locating objects by using sound waves that reflect off of the object or prey and return to the animal sending the sound waves.

herbivores: |erb-e-vors| Animals that eat only plants.

imprint: |im-print| To recognize as a parent.

navigate: |na-vi-gate| The ability of an animal to find its way over a long distance.

nocturnal: |nok-tur-nal| Active, awake, or occurring at night.

omnivores: |om-ne-vors| Animals that eat both plants and other animals.

regurgitate: |re-gur-ji-tate| To bring already swallowed food up again.

scavengers: |skav-enj-ers| Animals that find already-dead animals to eat.

sonar: |so-nar| A way to locate animals or objects in water by sending sound pulses that reflect back.

wattle: |wa-dle| A fleshy lobe hanging from the head or neck of some birds.

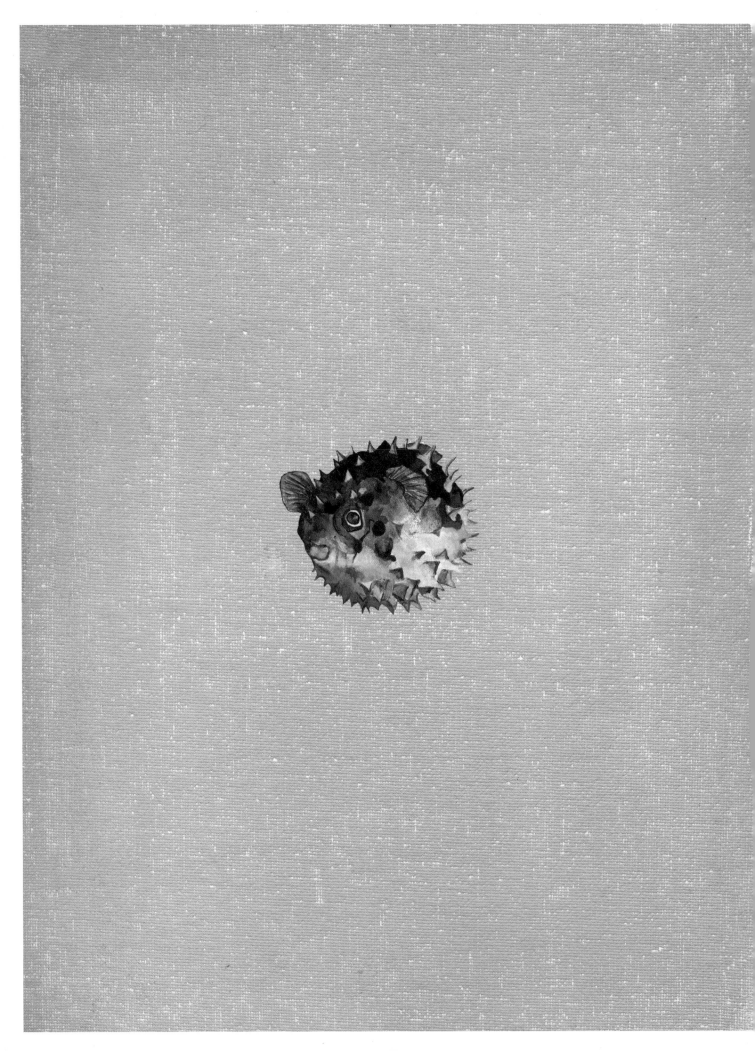